FreeFall

A Sea Turtle Falls From The Sky

Written by Lyn Littlefield Hoopes
Illustrated by Ray Bartkus

THE HUMANE SOCIETY OF THE UNITED STATES

for Melody and Woody,
in appreciation
~ Lyn Littlefield Hoopes

for my family
~ Ray Bartkus

Out of the blue
of a summer sky,
a tiny turtle falls,
flipping like a flap jack,
tumbling like a stone,
flapping its flippers
in the wind
all alone.

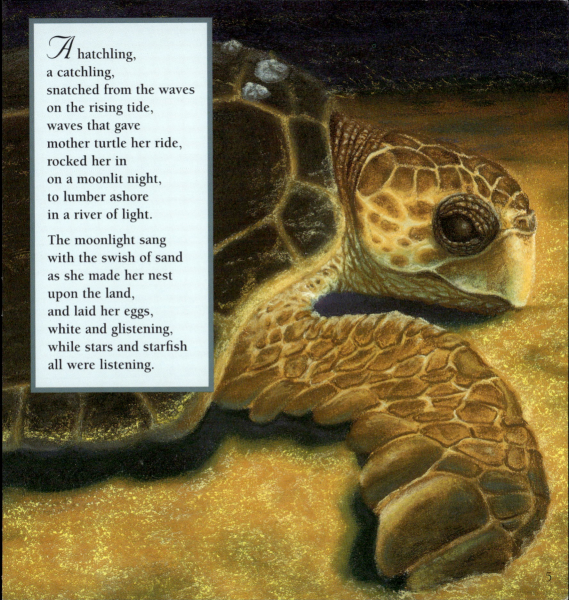

A hatchling,
a catchling,
snatched from the waves
on the rising tide,
waves that gave
mother turtle her ride,
rocked her in
on a moonlit night,
to lumber ashore
in a river of light.

The moonlight sang
with the swish of sand
as she made her nest
upon the land,
and laid her eggs,
white and glistening,
while stars and starfish
all were listening.

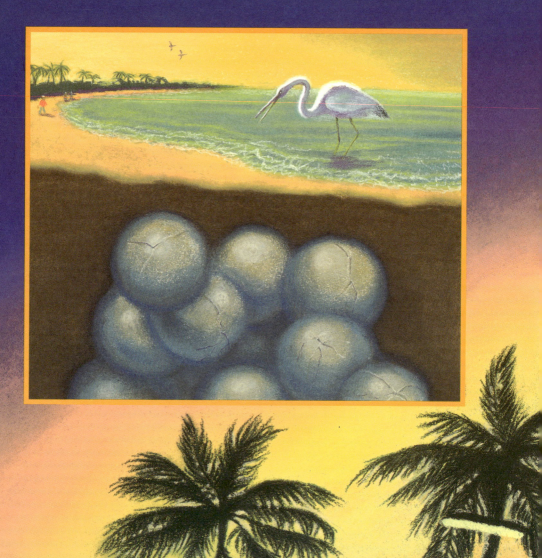

Out of the blue
of the summer sky
a tiny turtle falls...

a hatchling to fit
the palm of your hand.

Two months it grew
in a pocket of sand,
a nest of eggs
like ping pong balls.

Out of the sky,
a tiny turtle falls.

Down it sails
in a wild free fall,
just after hatching,
digging and scratching,
in a flurry, a hurry,
dashing to the sea.

One hundred tiny turtles
in a tiny turtle chase
raced ghost crab on the prowl,
raccoon and short-eared owl,
down to the waves
where the moonlight calls.

Out of the sky,
a tiny turtle falls.

'*Thwack!*'
Its a hatchling snatched
for a seagull snack,
swept up high
and dropped to crack,
a loggerhead turtle
shooting like a star,
landing with a 'smack'
on the hood of a car.

Sea turtles are rare;
all are endangered.
Out of thin air,
what could be stranger:
an ancient reptile
flipping its tail,
peering through a windshield
in Fort Lauderdale?

Tangled in nets
and strangled in trash,
mangled by props,
eggs stolen for cash,
the gentle sea turtle
that has lumbered ashore
since the early days
of the dinosaur,
in a wink, a blink,
may be extinct.

Steve Hall braked,
came to a stop,
leapt from his car
when he saw it drop.

One little turtle
with a scratch on her face,
a bent flipper,
and a bruised carapace,
would spend the night
in a bowl at his place.

As the moon rose,
the tiny turtle
began to doze.
The stars sparkling
out at sea
shone on her brothers
swimming free,
splashing to the sargassum weed,
where they would hide
and grow and feed.
One hundred hatchlings,
and only five
had made it out
past the gulls, alive.

The waves whispered
and the right whale cried:

Guard your flippers,
and you will glide.
You'll roam the seas
and journey deep;
sleep,
    tiny turtle,
        sleep.

$\mathcal{E}$arly in the morning
at the turn of the tide,
the tiny turtle
went for a ride,
up the escalator
by the visible nest,
past Clyde the alligator
taking a rest,
Boomer, the grouper,
and the puffer fish.
The tiny turtle
in a Tupperware dish
rode up in the Museum
of Discovery and Science,
where biologists are working
to save these ocean giants.

Woody, Melody,
Laura, and the vet
were quite surprised
by the turtle they met:
"Narrow escape!"
"Close call!"
"To survive alive
that wild free fall!"

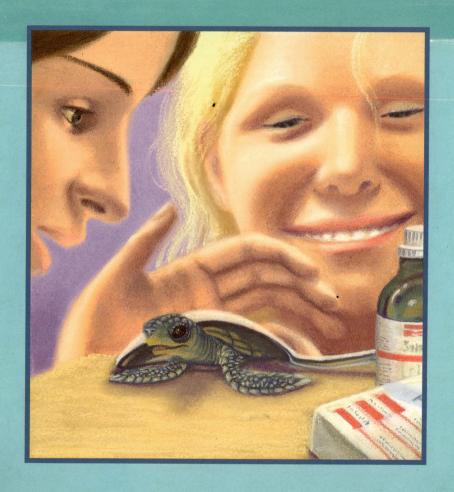

"Freefall! Freefall!"
Laura sang a tune
for a turtle that could hide
in a tablespoon.

One flipper was bent
and hung down low,
but she was heaven sent,
she would heal and grow.

She'd grow larger
than the hawksbills
and Kemp's ridleys,
larger than the flatbacks
of Australian seas.

She'd grow larger
than the green turtle,
larger than the black,
larger than all
but the leatherback.
In the nursery, she slept,
and not far outside,
the orca called
and the dolphins sighed:

*The seas you'll journey
are vast and deep,
You'll cross the ocean,
a promise to keep.
Guard your flippers,
your wings to fly,
deep in the wild, watery sky.*

𝓜elody is knocking
on Freefall's beak,
tucking a bite
in a tiny turtle cheek.
She pinches shrimp,
and gives it a wiggle,
way underwater,
a teasing jiggle.
Squid and crab:
she holds them low,
so Freefall will dive
and eat and grow.

Bit by bit,
Freefall gets stronger;
bite by bite,
she grows a little longer.
From a fifty cent piece
to a silver dollar,
she grows a little bolder,
...wider ...taller:
from the size of a saucer
to a salad plate.
Melody measures
and takes her weight.

Fall to winter,
winter to spring,
her dives grow deeper
and the manatees sing:

One night you'll rise
to a shore asleep,
climb the sand,
your promise to keep.

Guard your flippers,
and you will fly
deep in the wild, watery sky.

Freefall flaps a splash,
giving Woody a spank;
at six months old,
she's outgrown her tank.
With thorny spurs,
on each strong flipper,
she's going on exhibit
with her tank-mate, Skipper.

Down the escalator
by the visible nest,
where the hatchlings hatch,
Skipper grins for the guests.
Freefall swims
in her little ocean;
her flippers scissor
in an easy motion.

Cameras flash,
flippers splash.
Lips press kisses
to the glass.
Crowds of children
come to spy
the little sea turtle
that fell from the sky.

Amazed, they gaze
as Freefall sups,
circles, splashes,
hams it up.

She chases shrimp
and cracks crab claws,
grows a big block head
and powerful jaws,
the eyes of a clown
and a wrinkly chin,
a timid, toothless, old man's grin.

Spring to summer,
summer to fall,
they gather round
to see Freefall.

She spanks at the crowd:
they laugh in surprise
at an elfin face
with mischief in its eyes.

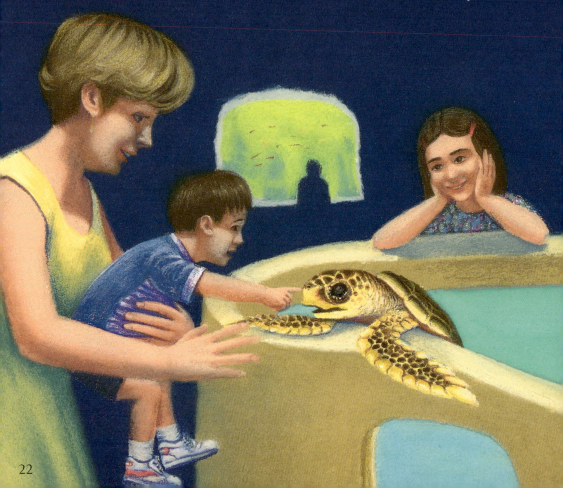

Mischief and secrets
and a promise to keep
to the moonlit ocean,
vast and deep,
its canyons to climb
and mountains to roam,
currents to carry her
on her way home,
home to mate,
to answer the call…

Freefall's tank is growing small.

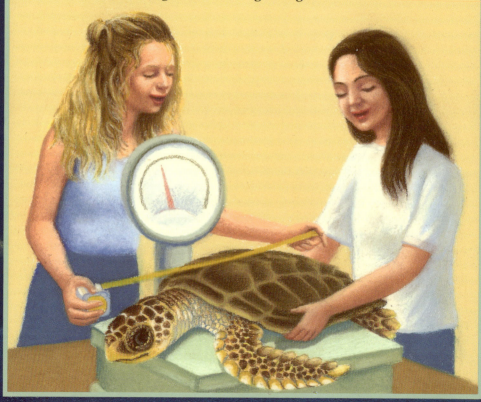

Week after week
as Freefall grows,
her tank shrinks,
her scissoring slows.

From the size of a plate
to a turkey platter –
she sleeps below now,
growing fatter.

Five,
>   ten,
>   fifteen,
>   twenty...
She's gained twenty pounds
in the year since hatching:
she's too big now
for seagull snatching.

Twenty-five,
>   thirty,
>   thirty-five,
>   forty...
forty-five and she's not slowing;
she'll weigh three hundred
and still be growing.

She's not yet ready
to battle the shark;
still her eyes are mysterious,
serious, dark.

An ancient promise
is hers to keep
to the ocean rolling
vast and deep,
to waves that gallop,
tossing their manes,
and whales in spouts
of silver rain,
to moonlit sand
and whispering foam...

Freefall now is going home.

$\mathcal{R}$oll the trolley
to her crate,
stop for a tag,
take her weight,
and she's off on her last ride,
off to catch the morning tide,
zipping away in Woody's van,
slipping away with a bunch of fans.
Cameramen, newsmen, turtlers all,
take to the road to free Freefall.

Her flippers are flapping,
spanking the air.
Melody, Laura,
Steve Hall are there,
each with a warning,
a silent wish:

*Plastic sacks
are not jellyfish…
trash will strangle,
nets entangle,
shore lights beckon
and misguide…
remember, they're not
the moon on the tide.
Beware the shark
and the man-o-war…*

Freefall wades out from the shore.

The waves whisper
their warning to stay,
to swim where its safe
in the shallow bay,
and the wind whistles
as right whales cry:

*Guard your flippers,
now you'll fly,
deep in the wild, watery sky.*

Out she splashes,
and dips below.
Where she swims,
no one can know.
But soon she rises
just offshore,
and flaps a flipper,
to dive once more.
Two spanks for thanks,
and she's out of sight,
leaving only a ripple
in the morning light.

*F*reefall!
The wind hums a tune
for a turtle who will rise
with the summer moon.

The sea will sing
with the swish of sand
as she makes her nest
upon the land,

and lays her eggs,
white and glistening,
while stars and starfish
all are listening,
while whales and moon snails
all are sleeping,
an ancient promise
she'll be keeping.

Glossary

Word	Page	Definition
Ancient	10	very old, from long ago
Beak	18	the bill of a turtle or bird
Beckon	27	call
Biologists	14	people who study the science of living things
Carapace	13	the hard shell covering a turtle's back
Elfin	22	like an elf or small mischief-making fairy
Endangered	10	very few left
Entangle	27	tie up
Extinct	10	all gone, none left
Flippers	2	broad, flat arms on a turtle
Glide	13	to move gently and smoothly
Glistening	5	shining brightly, wetly
Hatchling	5	an animal that has come out of an egg
Lumber	5	to move clumsily and slowly
Mischief	22	naughty playfulness
Misguide	27	lead astray
Props	10	propellers, blades of a motor on a boat (slang)
Prowl	8	to hunt for food
Reptile	10	type of animal, including turtles, snakes, lizards, alligators and crocodiles
Roam	13	go from place to place, wander
Sargassum Weed	13	a seaweed found in warmer parts of the Atlantic Ocean
Snatched	5	grabbed suddenly
Spurs	18	stiff, sharp spines
Trolley	27	a rolling cart on wheels
Turtlers	27	people who study turtles (slang)
Vast	17	very large, huge
Visible Nest	14	a nest that can be seen within a viewing box

the real Freefall

The mission of the Museum of Discovery and Science and the BLOCKBUSTER® IMAX® 3D Theater is to promote and increase the understanding and appreciation of science in children and adults through entertaining interaction with educational exhibits, programs, and films. As the highest attended museum of its kind in the state, the Museum opened its doors this past year to nearly 650,000 visitors. Formerly known as The Discovery Center, the 85,000 square-foot, $32.4 million museum opened its doors on November 21, 1992. The Museum is located at 401 SW Second Street, Fort Lauderdale, FL, 33312, and can be reached at (954) 467-6637.

The Humane Society of the United States was founded in 1954 to promote humane treatment of animals and to foster respect, understanding and compassion for all creatures and their enviornment. Up to 5% of the net wholesale price of this prodject goes to support The Humane Society. For more information, please write to: The HSUS, 2100 L Street, NW, Washington, DC 20037, or visit www.hsus.org.

Co-sponsorship of this book by The Humane Society of The United States does not imply any partnership, joint venture, or other direct affiliation between The HSUS and the Museum of Discovery and Science.

Text Copyright ©2000
Lyn Littlefield Hoopes
Illustrations Copyright © 2000
Ray Bartkus
Designed by Anita Soos Design, Inc.

Published by The Benefactory, Inc., 92 N. Milwaukee Avenue, Suite 101, Wheeling, IL 60090. The Benefactory produces books, tapes and toys that foster animal protection and enviornment preservation. For more information, call (847) 919-1777, or visit our website www.ReadPlay.com.